OF THIS EDITION OF "THE PASSING
OF THE ESSENES," FIVE HUNDRED
COPIES HAVE BEEN PRINTED FROM
TYPE AND THE TYPE DESTROYED.

THIS IS NUMBER 388

THE PASSING OF THE ESSENES

The PASSING of the ESSENES

A DRAMA IN THREE ACTS

By

GEORGE MOORE

New York

The Macmillan Company

1930

PRINTED IN THE UNITED STATES OF AMERICA

CHARACTERS *in the* PLAY

Jesus of Nazareth
Jacob, a young shepherd
Hazael, President of the Essenes
Mathias ⎫
Saddoc
Manahem
Caleb
Shallum ⎬ Essene monks
Eleazor
Eliakim
Bartholomew ⎭
Paul of Tarsus

SCENES

ACT I: Interior of the cenoby of the Essenes on a shelf of rock in the gorge of the brook Kerith. Evening.

ACT II: The same. Sunrise.

ACT III: The same. Later.

ACT I

The PASSING *of the* ESSENES

A C T I

SCENE: *The main hall of the cenoby of the Essenes, a rude, barn-like structure opening on to a balcony, on which there are seats. The* PRESIDENT'S *high-backed chair is on the right. Doors lead from the hall to the lecture-room and the cells.*

Enter JESUS, *with* JACOB, *a young shepherd. As they advance down the cave voices are heard.*

JACOB (*listening*)

WERE I out on the hills I'd say: Yoe bleateth after ram. Here my guess is that it is Mathias interpreting Scripture.

JESUS

Who then hath been talking to thee about Mathias, his voice and his doctrine?

JACOB

JACOB

Saddoc, whom I met the day I brought a
message from thee to the President. He was
sitting on the cliff's edge muttering: Heresies!
Heresies! and so deep was he in his thoughts
that a while went by before he understood
my question enough to answer: Hazael is with
the brethren, listening to Mathias proving the
Scriptures to be parables; and having said as
much he was off again. Adam and Eve, saith
he, could not have been so foolish as to hide
from God in a garden. Nobody hides from
God.

JESUS

Saddoc and Mathias are of different minds
about many things. Mathias, in truth, is hard
to understand, and is a great trouble to Saddoc.

JACOB

As this cavern will be to thee, Master; for
it will breed a great longing in thee for the sky
and the hills, the flock running merrily, follow-
ing after the sound of the pipe, the sunny
mornings on the hillsides and the oak wood
where we have sat so often resting through
the heats of midday. The drone from under
yon door will set thee thinking of Eliab, who
often soothed thee with sweet airs on the double
flute, or of Bozrah, who ran his fingers over
the strings of his harp to recall thee to us from
the

the dim heart of the wood. But it was in answer, methinks, to Havilah's pipe that thou wouldst come to the rugged oak; he had a lonely ditty that fetched thee. Ah, Master, thou canst not forget, so why leave us?

JESUS

Thou'rt right, Jacob. I have lived too long on the hills to forget them. I shall not seek to forget, and not many days will pass over without my coming to the hills to hearken to the sound of thy pipe. Mine I make over to thee.

JACOB

Thou must keep thy pipe, Master, to warn me of thy coming, and when I hear it I shall leap to my feet as the goat leaps at the sight of a quickening bough.

JESUS

I have taught thee much of my craft, Jacob.

JACOB

But Hazael will put questions to me that I cannot answer.

JESUS

Well, Hazael is without wit for sheep or goats.

JACOB

Hazael will say to thee: Jesus, thou must remain our shepherd till the next lambing season is over; and if he saith that he will say well.

JESUS

JESUS

It is not long since he said to me: Jesus, there is grey in thy beard; how old art thou? And when I answered: Fifty-three, his head sank on his breast and he muttered: And I have heard thee always spoken of as the boy Jesus.

JACOB

He would like to have thee with him, but he must think of the flock, and he will ask if the dogs will follow me.

JESUS

Thema takes meat from thee, and after a two-days' fast Gorbotha will come to thy call, and when they have run down a wolf or a jackal for thee, they'll know thee for their master. Take heed of thy flock. Do well the work that God hath given thee to do, remembering always that though the distance be great from bad pasture to good, the journey from the bad to the good will profit thee, though the flock be weary before they attain it; but however weary, if the grass be good they will fall to nibbling. And now, Jacob, before we part, remember that when the lambs are folded with the yoes thou'lt put into their jaws a stick to keep them from sucking; and keep thine eyes upon the lamb I pointed out to thee, for he will come into a fine, broad-shouldered ram, strong

across

across the loins and straight on his legs, the
sort to get lambs that will do well on these
hills; and thou'lt be wise to leave him for
another hundred days on his dam. Shear him,
for it will give him strength to take some wool
from him, but take it not from his back, for
he'll want the wool there to protect him from
the sun. All the first year he will skip about
the yoes and jump upon them, but it will be
only play, for his time is not yet come. In two
more years he will be at his height, serving
ten yoes a day; but keep him not overlong, for
thou must always have some new rams prepar-
ing, else the flock will decline. The ram that
I chose for thy lesson to-night is old and must
soon be replaced. He was a good ram in his
time, but the white ram that came at my call
is the best I have seen this many a year. The
white ram is stronger than the black, though
the black yoe will turn from him and seek a
ram of her own colour. I have known a white
ram so ardent for a black yoe that he fought
the black ram till their skulls cracked.

JACOB

But, Master——

[*The door of the lecture-room opens and*
MANAHEM *and* SADDOC *bear out* HAZAEL,
who has fainted. The ESSENES *are clad in
long white garments.*]

MANAHEM

MANAHEM (*as they cross the stage to
the balcony*)

As soon as we get him into the air he will
return to himself.

SADDOC

A little water!

[*Exit* JESUS. *He returns with water.* SADDOC
motions the others aside and bathes
HAZAEL'*s temples.*]

HAZAEL

The heat overcame me.   But I shall soon be
well, and then thou shalt bear me back to
hear——

SADDOC

Thou'lt do better to rest in the air of this
balcony.

HAZAEL

It was not the length of Mathias's discourse,
nor his eloquence, that caused my senses to
swoon away, but my age, which will not per-
mit me to listen long.   Hearken, Saddoc and
Manahem, I would be alone with Jesus, and do
you return to the lecture-room at once, else
our brother will be discouraged in his discourse.
Hasten, lest ye miss any more of his arguments.
[*The* ESSENES *are about to raise a protest, but
at a sign from* HAZAEL *they go out.*]   Who is
this standing by thee, Jesus?   Not one of the
brethren

brethren, for if he wore a white robe I should
see it.

JESUS

It is Jacob. I have brought him this evening
to receive thy commands. To-night I remain
with thee here.

HAZAEL

So thou biddest the hills farewell to-night?

JESUS

Why not to-night, since I am bringing thee
a shepherd who will serve thee as well as I
have served thee? Another may claim him
whilst the winter lasts, for his fame is spread-
ing.

HAZAEL

Thy master speaks well of thee, Jacob.

JACOB

He speaks too well of me, sir. I had ill luck
on the hills over against Cæsarea.

JESUS (*to* HAZAEL)

He went thither in search of pasture, for
tidings reached Kerith that rain had fallen in
the west.

JACOB

I had no dogs, Master. Let Hazael know
that my dogs were taken the night before by
panthers.

JESUS

There is nothing so toothsome to a panther
as a dog; he will risk his life fearlessly for one.

And

And how many wolves were there, Jacob, in the pack that trailed thee?

Jacob

Ten or a dozen, and what defence would my poor dogs have been against a pack like that? 'Twas the fourth night, and I could not find the cavern I looked for and lay down in the open with my flock. . . . After the loss of my flock I lived as I could on the scraps the shepherds threw me. But they wearied of charity, and I'd be sitting now with the lepers by the wayside above Jericho if Jesus had not given his lambs into my charge.

Jesus

Jacob lost faith in himself, as we all do at times.

Jacob

I am young, said I to myself, and can wait. Jesus, who knows more than all the other shepherds together, holds me to be no fool. I am young and can wait, and who knows, Jesus may tell me his cure for the scab, and by serving him I may get a puppy when Thema litters.

Hazael

Jacob, it is for thee to listen rather than to speak, and since Jesus believes that thou canst replace him, the flock from henceforth is in thy charge.

[Jesus *goes up the stage with* Jacob]

Jesus

JESUS

Thou'lt come to fetch me in the morning; we'll count the sheep together. And take heart, Jacob, for I shall always be by in case of need.

JACOB

Am I to feed the dogs, Master?

JESUS

To-morrow they'll take food from thee at my bidding as before.

[*Exit* JACOB]

HAZAEL

I gave Caleb a letter this morning for thee, charging him to search the hills.

JESUS

After reading thy letter I held my peace with Jacob, and it was not till the last yoe was made clean for the winter that I said to him: I have come to the end of my life on the hills. He was frightened at the thought of leaving me before the lambing-time——

HAZAEL

And I am frightened at the thought of leaving thee before the springtime. I shall be sorry to leave thee, Jesus, for our lives have been twisted together, strands of the same rope. But it must be plain to thee that I am growing weaker; month by month, week by week, my strength is ebbing; I am going out. But for what reason should I lament that God hath not

chosen

chosen to retain me for a few months longer,
since my life cannot be prolonged for more than
a few months? My eighty and odd years have
left me with barely strength enough to sit in
the doorway looking back on the way I have
come. Every day the things of this world grow
fainter and life becomes to me an unreal thing,
and myself becomes unreal to those around me.
Only for thee do I retain anything of my
vanished self. So why should I remain? For
thy sake, lest thou be lonely here? Well, that
is reason enough, and I will bear the burden of
life as well as I can for thy sake. A burden it
is, and for a reason that thou mayst not divine,
for thou art still a young man in my eyes, and,
moreover, hast not lived under a roof year after
year listening to learned interpretations of the
Scriptures. Thou hast not guessed, nor wilt
thou ever guess till age reveals it to thee, that
as we grow old we do not love God as once we
loved him. No one would have thought, not
even thou, who art more conscious of God's
presence than any one under this roof, I say
not even thou wouldst have thought that as we
approach death our love of God grows weaker,
but this is so. In great age nothing seems to
matter, and it is from this indifference that I
wish to escape. Thou goest forth in the morning to lead thy flock in search of pasture, and
God

God is nearer to us in the wilderness than he is among men.

JESUS

Art afraid that under this roof I, too, may cease to love God?

HAZAEL

Not cease to love God.

JESUS

Thou wouldst warn me that God is loved only on the hills under the sky?

HAZAEL

I am too weak to choose my thoughts or words, and many things pass out of my mind. Had I remembered I would not have spoken.

JESUS

But why not speak, Father? for I would be ready to resist the changes that may befall.

HAZAEL

Only this can I say with certainty, Jesus, that the sky will always be before thine eyes and the green fields under thy feet, yea, even whilst listening to Mathias.

JESUS

Thou, too, didst live once under the sky.

HAZAEL

In beforetimes the love of God was ardent in me, and whether walking by day or by night I was always watchful for the young man in whom I might discover an Essene for Kerith. But

But, Jesus, why this grief? Because I am going from thee? Dear friend, to come and go is the law of life, and perchance I shall be with thee longer than thou thinkest. Eighty and odd years may be lengthened into ninety; the patriarchs lived till a hundred and more years, and we believe that the soul outlives the body. Out of the chrysalis we escape from our corruptible bodies, and the beautiful butterfly flutters Godward. Grieve for me a little when I am gone, but grieve not before I go, for I would see thy face always happy, as I remember it in those years long ago in Nazareth. Jesus, Jesus, thou shouldst not weep like this! None should weep but for sin, and thy life is known to me from the day in Nazareth when we sat in the street together to the day that thou wentest to the Jordan to get baptism from John.

JESUS

A year of my life is unknown to thee, Hazael.

HAZAEL

We will not speak of it, nor of thy transgression of our rules, atoned for on the hills. Since God hath forgiven thee, why should we be laggards in forgiveness?

JESUS

I pray thee, say not another word, Hazael, for none is less worthy than I. The greatest

sinner

sinner amongst us is sitting by thee, one that
hath not dared to tell his secret to thee for
twenty years or more.

HAZAEL

On thy return to us thou wouldst have told
all that befell thee in Galilee, but neither I nor
the brethren wished to hear thy story.

JESUS

John's doctrine of repentance entered into my
life and I preached it, but little by little——

HAZAEL

Jesus, I beseech thee! Twenty years agone
it was decided that we should not question thee.
We were certain that thy hand had done no
wrong and that no sinful thought ever entered
thy mind.

JESUS

I lacked courage——

HAZAEL

No, Jesus, thy conscience deceives thee.
Courage was not lacking. But we did not wish
to hear thee, and thou, in thy great kindness,
forbore for our sakes to speak.

JESUS

I said then that I could not come to live
among you without confessing my sins, and
went to the hills to lead my flock. And now
that I have come again to live with you, the
quiet and peace that I seek would be far away
if——

HAZAEL

HAZAEL

If thou didst not tell all the scruples that
infect thee. But, Jesus, more than ever I beg
that thou wilt not disturb the cenoby with
confessions of past sins, tribulations and doubts.
Silence is required of thee. Twenty years agone
we were content with the Scriptures and with
the rules of our Order. Questions were not
rife. But ever since Mathias came from Egypt
and read the Scriptures differently from Saddoc,
finding allegories everywhere, all is changed.
Some of our brethren, feeling that the solitude
of Kerith was not enough, sought a deeper
solitude in the clefts above us. Whatever may
have befallen thee in Galilee, and afterwards
in Jerusalem, would set the cenoby aflame with
violent discussion were it disclosed now. Ha-
treds would spring up, and the desire to escape.

JESUS

Are there then brethren amongst us who
would break their vows?

HAZAEL

I say naught against any brother, but there is
disquiet. I had looked forward to a peaceful
old age, with thee beside me. Shatter it not with
disclosures, whatever they may be. [*Pause.*]

JESUS

I am too old to follow the flock any longer
on the hills. I have done my best with it, and
have

have given it in good condition to Jacob. There
is reason in what thou sayest, Hazael. I would
not disturb the peace of thy last years, and if I
come to live with thee, and accept thy guid-
ance, my first duty is obedience.

[*The door of the lecture-room opens and the*
    ESSENES *come out singing:*]
In the Lord put I my trust:
How say ye to my soul, Flee
As a bird to your mountain?
For, lo, the wicked bend their
Bow, they make ready their arrow
Upon the string, that they may privily
Shoot at the upright in heart.
If the foundations be destroyed, what
Can the righteous do?
For the righteous Lord loveth
Righteousness; his countenance
Doth behold the upright.

JESUS

These words of the Psalmist were meant for
me, and now that the brethren are here I may
not speak. But to-morrow——

HAZAEL

There may be no to-morrow for me. [*To
the* ESSENES.] Our brother Jesus hath given
over the charge of our flocks to a young shepherd.

SADDOC

All the cells, Father, are filled.   HAZAEL

HAZAEL

Jesus can sleep here on this bench. A mattress and a cloak will be enough for him who hath slept in caverns or in valleys on stones piled high to keep him above the floods. Manahem will get thee a mattress, Jesus; he knows where to find one. [*Exit* MANAHEM.] I am strong enough to walk alone, Saddoc. [*He disengages himself from* SADDOC's *arm and walks with the* ESSENES *towards his cell, joining them in the psalm:*]

All the powers of the Lord
Bless ye the Lord; praise and
Exalt him above all for ever.

[*Exeunt* HAZAEL *and the* ESSENES. SADDOC *remains with* JESUS.]

SADDOC

The brethren are weary of hearing Mathias prove that the Scriptures are but allegories, and for a long time have been talking of thee, saying: He'll come back with stories of the robbers he hath met and the wolves and the bears he hath escaped. True enough, there are some that would have thee stay on the hills, for thy Jacob, not being one of us, will claim one lamb out of every twenty, and these he may send to the temple for burnt-offerings, the which, as thou knowest, is forbidden by our laws. I have much more

to

to tell, but here Manahem comes with a mattress for thee.

[*Enter* MANAHEM *carrying a mattress.*]
MANAHEM

Wilt thou sleep, Jesus, within the cavern, or on the balcony under the sky?

JESUS

On the balcony, dear brother.

SADDOC (*helping* MANAHEM *to lay the mattress on the balcony*)

On this bench he will lie comfortably under a covering, for though the evenings are still warm the nights are chilly. Fetch a warm covering, Manahem. [*Exit* MANAHEM. SADDOC *approaches* JESUS.] Since Mathias came we have never had an easy day with our own thoughts. What dost thou think he was saying when we returned to the lecture-room?

JESUS

I cannot read the mind of Mathias, Saddoc.

SADDOC

That there are two beings in man, one that hath prudence and the other that exerts it; and he doth liken these two principles to a carbuncle and an emerald!

[*Enter* MANAHEM *with a quilt.*]
MANAHEM

The warmest I could find, perhaps too warm.

JESUS

JESUS (*feeling the quilt*)

My thanks, brother, my thanks. [*He passes to the farther end of the balcony and leans on the rail.*] How still the night is, not a sound in it but the murmur of the brook flowing down the gorge to Jordan. . . . Ye have voices of wayfarers sometimes at your door asking for shelter and bread?

SADDOC

The dangers of the path save us from wayfarers.

MANAHEM

Once on a time a wayfarer dared to follow the path by night, and he lost his life over the cliffs in the brook.

JESUS

Come, Manahem, and tell me if thine eyes discern not a man in the path yonder.

MANAHEM

I see none.

JESUS

Look again, Manahem.

SADDOC (*going to the balcony*)

Truly, our shepherd's eyes are better than ours. A man is on the path, trying to follow it, and if he be a man of flesh and blood like ourselves, he will topple.

MANAHEM

He hath not yet gone over into the brook, but

but keeps the path as if he knew it. He is maybe one of our dissident brothers come up from Jordan.

SADDOC

Now he is crossing the bridge, and now he begins the ascent. Let us pray that he may miss the path through the terraces.

JESUS

But thou wouldst not have him miss it, Saddoc? He shall have my mattress.

SADDOC

If not an evil spirit, of a certainty he is coming to ask for shelter for the night. And if not a demon, he may be a prophet or a robber; for once more the hills are filled with robbers.

JESUS

Or it may be the preacher of whom Jacob spoke to me this evening. He came up from Jordan with a story of a preacher that the multitude would not listen to and sought to drown in the river; and he told me how the rabble had followed the man over the hills with intent to kill him.

MANAHEM

Some great and terrible heresy he must be preaching to stir them like that. Did Jacob bring news of his escape or death?

JESUS

He thought the prophet must have escaped
into

into a cave, for he came upon the crowd going home like dogs from a hunt when they have lost their quarry.

SADDOC

A robber is at our door, for sure. He escaped the crowd and hath been hiding in a cave. Only a robber who knew the hills could have kept the path. . . . Now he sees us! He is no shepherd, but a robber. [*They wait a few moments, and the knocking they expect comes at the door.*] Open not the door, Jesus! There are Sicarii who kill men in the daytime, mingling themselves among the multitude with daggers hidden in their garments, their mission being to stab those that disobey the law in any fraction. We are Essenes and may not send blood offerings to the temple. Open not the door! Sicarii or Zealots travel in search of heretics through the cities of Samaria and Judea. Open not the door! Men are for ever fooled, and will never cease to open their doors to those who stand in need of meat and drink. It will be safer, Jesus, to bid him away. Tell him rather that we'll let down a basket of meat and drink from the balcony to him.

JESUS

Art thou, Manahem, for turning this man from the door or letting him in?

MANAHEM

MANAHEM

There is no need to be frightened. He is
but a wanderer, Saddoc.

SADDOC

A wanderer he cannot be, for he hath
followed the path through the darkness, a
thing we could not do. Open not the door,
I tell thee, else we all hang on crosses above
the hills to-morrow. [*He goes to the door and
listens.*]

MANAHEM

But, Saddoc, by our law we may not refuse
bed and board to the poor.

JESUS

If we do not open he will leave our door,
and that will be a greater misfortune than any
he may bring us. Hearken, Saddoc!

SADDOC (*to* MANAHEM)

He speaks fair enough. But we may plead
that after sunset in the times we live in——

JESUS

Manahem, art thou with me or with Saddoc?
We know that there is but one man, and we
are more than a match for one. Put a sword
in Saddoc's hand.

SADDOC

No, Manahem! I should feel like a fool
with a sword in my hand. Since thou sayest,
Jesus, there is but one man, and we are three,

it

it might be unlucky to turn him from our door.

JESUS

May I then open to him?

[JESUS *unbars the door, and* PAUL *staggers in, bald-headed, his turban having fallen in his flight. He is a powerful man of medium height, with broad shoulders, piercing black eyes, shaggy eyebrows, and a hooked nose. A black beard covers the lower part of his face. He stands like a hunted animal, breathing hard, looking from one to the other.*]

PAUL

May I rest a little while? If so, give me to drink before I sleep. No food, but drink. Why do ye not answer? Do ye fear me, mistaking me for a robber? Or have I wandered among robbers? Where am I? [*To* JESUS.] Hearken, I am but a wayfarer, and thou'rt a shepherd of the hills—I know thee by thy garb. Thou'lt not refuse me shelter?

JESUS (*to* SADDOC *and* MANAHEM)

He shall have the mattress I was to sleep upon. [*To* PAUL.] Thou shalt have food and a coverlet.

PAUL

No food, but a drink of water.

SADDOC

SADDOC

There is some yoes' milk on the shelf,
Manahem.

[MANAHEM *fetches the milk, which* PAUL
drinks greedily.]

JESUS (*to* PAUL)

I'll get thee a linen garment; sleep will
come easier in it; and I'll bathe thy feet.

[*Exit* JESUS.]

PAUL

A shepherd told me that after I had passed
the bridge I'd find terraces leading upwards
to this ledge of rock.

MANAHEM

We watched thee from the balcony. At
every step we feared thou wouldst topple out
of the path into the abyss.

SADDOC

If the shepherd hath told thee that we in
this cavern are of the Essenes, and that no
traveller was ever turned from our door, he
hath told thee truly. But we would know
whom we are guesting.

PAUL

I am Paul of Tarsus, a prisoner of the
Romans——

SADDOC

A prisoner of the Romans! [*To* MANA-
HEM.] Mayhap with soldiers at his heels!

Let

Let us put him beyond the door.   Manahem,
aid me!

> [SADDOC *tries to drag* PAUL *to his feet.*
> JESUS *enters, with a basin of water and a
> garment.*]

JESUS

Are we not forbidden by our rule to thrust
a stranger from our door?

SADDOC

But he tells us he is a prisoner of the
Romans.

JESUS

Even so, we cannot turn him away to fall
into the abyss.

SADDOC

He kept to the path on his way hither
and will doubtless return by it safely to the
hills.

PAUL (*to* JESUS)

I am not a criminal fleeing from the
Romans, but a Roman citizen escaping from
Jewish persecution.

SADDOC

Why, then, didst thou say thou wert a
prisoner of the Romans?

PAUL

I am a prisoner of the Romans for a riot
that began two years ago in Jerusalem, whither
a great pressing of the spirit urged me, for I
would

would not leave Asia before preaching once
more in Jerusalem to the Jews, a stiff-necked,
gainsaying race, but dear to me despite its
stubbornness. But the people were stirred up
against me, and would have stoned me had
not the Roman guard come out to quell the
uproar and borne me on their shoulders up the
steps of the castle, whither the people thronged
after me, rending their garments, throwing
dust in the air, crying: Away with him for the
scourging! As I was being bound I turned to
the centurion and asked him if it were lawful
to scourge a Roman citizen and he untried;
whereupon they desisted, and I was sent to
Cæsarea to be judged. And the Jews, still
thirsting for my blood, sent elders from the
temple to Festus, saying: We would question
this man in Jerusalem on some points of the
law; give him over to us. But I said to the
noble Festus: These men are planning to kill
me in an ambush; I appeal to Cæsar. And he
answered me: Thou hast appealed to Cæsar,
and to Cæsar thou shalt go. But the ship
that was to take me to Rome was delayed,
and a great pressing of the spirit came upon
me to preach in Jericho, for I was loth to
leave many Jews without knowledge of the
Lord Jesus. And the noble Festus said to me:
Go then to Jericho and preach thy doctrine,
but

but I shall expect thee back within six days.

SADDOC

And how was thy doctrine received in Jericho?

PAUL

With stones, from which I escaped through the hills. But of all this I will tell ye to-morrow. Do ye tell me now of a young man, Timothy, who followed me along the cliff.

JESUS

Thou wast alone.

SADDOC (*whispering to* MANAHEM)

He must have preached some terrible heresy for the Jews to seek his life with stones.

PAUL

Should Timothy have fallen into the hands of the Jews he is lost to me for ever.

JESUS

We know not of whom thou art speaking.

PAUL (*rising*)

Of Timothy, my son in the faith, who missed me where the hillside tumbles into shale and rubble and the road disappears. I must go in search of him.

JESUS

God hath upheld thee in a dangerous path for his purposes, and thou art welcome to remain with us for the night.

PAUL

PAUL

Thy thought is that Timothy would be sought in vain in the darkness.

[JESUS *unties* PAUL'S *sandals and bathes his feet.*]

SADDOC

Since thou art guesting among us we would hear more of the great pressing of the spirit that bade thee to Jericho.

PAUL

To preach the Lord Jesus, the Messiah promised to the Jews, who was raised from the dead. But the people would not listen.

MANAHEM

And why would they not listen? for 'tis not every day a tale is told of a man being raised from the dead.

PAUL

Stirred up by the priests the many sought to capture us; but we escaped into the hills and hid in a cave to which the spirit of the Lord directed us.

MANAHEM (*whispering to* SADDOC)

Hark, an angel pointed out a cave to him!

SADDOC

Mayhap an angel did, but whether a good or an evil angel we know not.

[JESUS *relieves* PAUL *of his garment and passes a white robe over his shoulders.*]

PAUL

PAUL

Jericho would have done well to hearken to me, for have I not testified in many synagogues of the great light that blinded me on the road to Damascus, and the voice that cried to me out of the clouds: Saul, Saul, why persecutest thou me?

[*Consciousness passes from* PAUL. *He falls back in the arms of* JESUS *and* SADDOC.]

SADDOC

Of what is he telling us?

JESUS

He hath fallen asleep. Help me to lift him to a couch on the balcony.

[JESUS *and* SADDOC *carry* PAUL *to the balcony and lay him on one of the benches. They cover him with a quilt.* JESUS *lies down beside him on another bench.* SADDOC *returns to* MANAHEM.]

MANAHEM

Now, what did he say before he fell asleep?

SADDOC

He was telling us that on the road to Damascus a voice cried to him out of the clouds. [*They move a little nearer to* PAUL.] A heavy man to carry and to lift on to a couch.

MANAHEM

He spoke of many things besides Damascus.

SADDOC

SADDOC

He did; but words pass out of the mind
quickly. I recall that the Jews drove him out
of Jericho with stones, and that he lost his
son in the faith, Timothy, on the hillside.

MANAHEM

His very words.

SADDOC

Had I had my wits about me I'd have asked
him if his doctrine came out of the Scriptures.

MANAHEM

He was too weary to tell it plainly.

SADDOC

And we shall stumble when we try to tell it
to the brethren. Let us go over it together.

MANAHEM

Mathias will put cunning questions to him.
A rare occasion it will be for the Egyptian to
entangle him and press him into evasions and
contradictions.

SADDOC

Mathias will resolve the story of the voice
speaking out of the clouds into allegory.

MANAHEM

In truth, whatever befell, his account of it is
nowise clear.

SADDOC

He said the Lord Jesus was raised from the
dead. Said he not so, Manahem?

MANAHEM

MANAHEM

He said many things, speaking like a man in a dream.

SADDOC

Try to recall if he were stoned because of a heresy.

MANAHEM

I barely remember. . . . My thoughts are dim and treacherous, but at daybreak the mind is clear.

[*Exit* MANAHEM. SADDOC *returns to the balcony, looks anxiously at* PAUL *and goes out.*]

CURTAIN

ACT II

A C T I I

SCENE: *The same. Sunrise. When the curtain rises a shepherd's pipe is heard from afar. A slight interval, and the pipe is heard again, this time much nearer.* PAUL *and* JESUS *are asleep on benches on either side of the balcony. Neither awakes.*

JACOB *appears at the end of the gallery. He advances cautiously. He is about to play his pipe again with a view to awakening the sleepers. He hesitates, decides not to do so, and advances towards them. Touching* JESUS *with his pipe he awakens him.* JESUS *rises to his feet and signs to* JACOB *that he is not to speak.* JESUS *and* JACOB *come down the stage.*

JACOB

S O the preacher found his way into the cenoby!

JESUS

A great knocking came at our door, and I gave him the bed that Manahem and Saddoc were making for me.

JACOB

JACOB

But his fellow—where is he?

JESUS

He asked for his fellow, and would have gone in search of him. But he fell asleep in our arms whilst talking.

JACOB

At daybreak it was reported that the twain escaped through a swirl of water that no man would have dared his life into but to save it. On seeing them carried down to the sea, the people laughed and clapped their hands, saying: They will drink of bitterness before they drown, and if they drown not we shall take them in Moab. But they kept to the bank they plunged from, and belike a sudden flux in the current carried them up a shelving strand, whence they escaped into the hills.

JESUS

We can get this man to Cæsarea by crossways known only to us.

JACOB

We can indeed; and be sure I'll lead him to safety, Master.

JESUS

An evil blow might befall thee, or many stripes, or a stoning.

JACOB

JACOB

I owe thee my life, and thine being worth
twenty such lives as mine——

JESUS

I am but a shepherd on the hills of Kerith
like thyself.

JACOB

Thou art above us, Master, and always in
our thoughts, whether we speak of sheep or of
the sick. Of what art thou thinking? I said
yesterday to a man, and got from him the story
of the ram Cæsar, brought by thee from Cæsarea, the original Adam of the flock. And
when he heard from me that thou wert about
to bid the hills farewell, he sighed and began
the story of his wife, who was bed-rid for three
years and would be so still if thou hadst not
called to her from the doorway: Woman, rise
and gown thyself! The sick ask for something
thou hast touched—the laces from thy shoe, a
strip from a veil thou hast worn. We cannot
spare thee, Master.

JESUS

Come with me into the hills to warn the
shepherds that should a strange man come to
them asking for direction to Cæsarea, they must
guide him and give him bread and drink, and
sandals, should he need them.

[JESUS *and* JACOB *go up the stage, and* SAD-
DOC

DOC *and* MANAHEM *enter, followed by* CALEB *carrying bread and a jug of milk.*]

JESUS (*to the* ESSENES)

Our guest still sleeps. Do not awaken him, and when his eyes open tell him that I have gone in search of his fellow and will return to guide him to Cæsarea.

[*Exeunt* JESUS *and* JACOB. *The* ESSENES *approach* PAUL.]

CALEB

He sleeps like one whom naught could awake but the trumpets of Judgment.

SADDOC

I would he were away. He hath had his rest, and I am mindful of the great danger it is to hide a man alike an enemy of the Jews and Romans.

[PAUL *awakes, and seeing the three figures looks round with staring eyes, like one who believes himself to be the victim of an hallucination.*]

PAUL (*rising to his feet*)

Who are ye? And where am I? Yonder is daylight. . . . I must escape!

MANAHEM

Hast forgotten knocking at our door last night?

PAUL

Last night I was swimming in Jordan and
escaped

escaped through the hills. . . . I shall disentangle it all presently. . . . But Timothy, my son in the faith—where is he?

MANAHEM

The shepherd who slept by thee hath gone in search of thy fellow.

PAUL (*trying to recover himself*)

When my eyes opened and I saw you in your white garments . . .

CALEB

I bring thee bread and a jug of milk freshly drawn.

[PAUL *drinks*.]

PAUL

My feet pain me.

MANAHEM

Jesus, our shepherd, bathed them. Hast forgotten?

PAUL

No. He gave me a garment, saying I would sleep easier in it.

[*Exit* CALEB.]

MANAHEM

The rule of our Order is to succour the tired traveller.

PAUL

And assuredly I was one last night.

[*He begins to eat the bread, and whilst he is eating* MATHIAS *enters, followed by* SHALLUM, ELEAZOR, ELIAKIM, BARTHOLOMEW,

THOLOMEW, *and* CALEB, *who carries a plate of lentils. Seeing that* PAUL *is eating* CALEB *whispers to* BARTHOLOMEW, *who goes out and returns with a small table, which he places before* PAUL.]

CALEB (*laying the plate on the table*)

Lentils boiled in water is our fare, but our rule allows butter to our guests.

MATHIAS (*to* PAUL)

Our President will be ready to speak with thee before midday and will press thee to remain with us till thou hast regained enough strength to continue thy journey.

[*The* ESSENES *make a movement of withdrawal.*]

PAUL

A few hours' sleep is enough for a hardened wayfarer like me. Stay, noble Essenes. I thank you for the rest I have had, and for the delay that your President would press upon me; but I am under bond to return to Cæsarea to go on board the ship that will take me to Rome.

MANAHEM (*to* MATHIAS)

Our guest hath appealed to Cæsar.

MATHIAS (*to* PAUL)

Thou art then a rich man, who paid a great sum of money for thy citizenship?

PAUL

PAUL

My citizenship was not purchased. I was born free.

MATHIAS

Yet thou art at enmity with Jews and Romans alike.

PAUL

A prisoner of the Romans for a riot in Jerusalem, and hated of the Jews for I preach a new dispensation, but an enemy of no man, rather the friend of all men.

CALEB

We would hear of this riot in Jerusalem.

MATHIAS

He hath come to rest, not to tell stories.

CALEB

But is he to leave us without knowledge of the Lord Jesus? Manahem and Saddoc had the story overnight. Are we not to hear it?

MATHIAS

What sayest thou, Saddoc?

SADDOC

That I'd liefer see the man eat his lentils than listen to him telling stories of the Lord Jesus.

CALEB

Paul is leaving us at midday, and we would not forgo the story he tells.

BARTHOLOMEW

Of the man raised from the dead.

MANAHEM

MANAHEM

The first of all mankind to escape death.

MATHIAS

Elijah was spared death.

MANAHEM

A miracle—no man denies it; but a greater miracle was the raising of the Lord Jesus from the dead.

PAUL

God loves his creations—this earth and the men upon it, wherefore he sent his only be-gotten son to suffer death on the cross that all men might believe and be saved.   And the Jews being a stiff-necked race, he decreed that the birth of the Lord Jesus should be as miraculous as his resurrection.   He was born of a virgin.

MATHIAS

In the absence of our President——

PAUL (*rising to his feet*)

I leave at midday, but I would not withhold from the Essene brotherhood the story of the Lord Jesus.

SHALLUM

We would hear it!

PAUL

Time, always on the march, will allow but a fragment——

SEVERAL ESSENES

Speak! Speak!

[*The*

[*The* ESSENES *fetch seats and range them-*
selves round PAUL, *who speaks from be-*
hind the table.]

PAUL

Learn then that I am Paul of Tarsus, a
Hebrew like yourselves, beforetimes a Pharisee
standing by the law, obeying it and hating
those who denied it or questioned it.   Such a
manner of man I was in the city of Tarsus,
a tent-maker, clever at the loom and learned
in the Scriptures.

MATHIAS

I would warn our President——

ELEAZOR (*detaining him*)

Stay! Stay!

SADDOC

If thou leavest us, Mathias, who will trip
up this wandering soothsayer when he reasons
falsely?

ELIAKIM

If to listen to him be a breach of the
law——

SADDOC

We were afraid to open the door to him——

PAUL

Mistaking me for a robber!

BARTHOLOMEW

On with the story!

ELEAZOR

We would hear it!   We would hear it!

PAUL

PAUL

One day there came to Tarsus tidings that a man was preaching in every town and village in Galilee that the end was come of the law given to Moses and the Prophets, and the promise given in its stead of eternal happiness for Jews and Gentiles alike. I was wroth indeed, and went about asking if there was nobody with authority to confute this man and cast him into prison, to bind him with chains, and if needs be, to flog him with rods. Further news of the man Jesus came to Tarsus, of the Apostles he had gathered round him, and of the crowds that accepted his promises of the new dispensation that God had vouchsafed to his people. My rage increased, and then the news came that the man Jesus had been seized by order of the High Priest and crucified. More than that I knew not, and urged by a great pressing of the spirit I left Tarsus, and in the streets of Jerusalem beheld the first martyr, Stephen, stoned by the populace, a sight that gave me great joy. One heretic the less! I said, and went to the High Priest to ask for letters that would give me the right to arrest all ill thinkers and lead them back in chains to Jerusalem. But when we came in view of Damascus, and saw the roofs between the trees, I heard a voice crying to me: Saul, Saul

Saul, why persecutest thou me? It is hard for
thee to kick against the pricks. And trem-
bling I fell forward, my face upon the ground.
The voice continued: I am Jesus whom thou
persecutest. Arise and go into the city, and it
shall be told to thee what thou must do. My
followers, who were but stricken and not
blinded as I was, took me by the arm and led me
into Damascus, where I abode as a blind man
till Ananias laid his hands upon me and the
scales fell from my eyes and I cried out for
baptism; and having received baptism, which
is spiritual strength, and taken food, which is
bodily, I went up to the synagogue to preach
the passing of the old world, till the Jews of
the city rose up against me and would have
killed me if I had not escaped them, let down
from the wall in a basket.

SHALLUM

From a window?

PAUL

From a window, in drenching rain and in
darkness, carried many times by the wind
against the wall. But I escaped from Damascus and went into Arabia to take counsel with
myself, for I could not doubt that the Lord
Jesus, speaking out of the clouds, had appointed
me his Apostle and established my authority
above that of Peter or John or James, or any
of

of the twelve who walked with him in Galilee. All the same, I could not forget Stephen, whose death I had witnessed in the streets of Jerusalem, and my words: One heretic the less! and I was tortured by a memory of my journey to Damascus, whither I had gone to persecute the Saints. But my doubts were assuaged by the Lord Jesus, and I learned that the words spoken to me out of the clouds were not intended for me alone, but for all the world.

CALEB

Did the Lord Jesus speak to thee again out of the clouds?

MATHIAS

There are few clouds in Arabia, Caleb.

PAUL

God liveth above the clouds, wherefore he speaks out of them. My doctrine was not born of the imaginations of my heart, but given unto me by the Lord Jesus in Arabia. From Arabia I went up to Jerusalem to speak with them that were in the city when the Lord was crucified, and it was Barnabas who brought me to Peter, saying that albeit I had persecuted, I was now zealous in the faith and had preached in many synagogues that Christ Jesus had died and been raised from the dead. Paul, said Barnabas, hath come from Arabia to hear the story of the Lord Jesus from thee, and Peter answered

answered: That story I will tell willingly to
whosoever asketh it of me, for it is a story of
exceeding worth to men. And he told that
one day, distracted with grief, his wife being
nigh to death, he rushed out of the house to
bring a physician, and meeting with a man
coming up from the lake, and mistaking him
for a physician, his grief being such that he
had no eyes for his torn garment, he said:
Come thou to my house; impose thy hands
and bid my wife rise from her bed and walk.
I will do this, Jesus answered, but he charged
Peter not to believe all he heard about him,
nor to speak of what might happen in his
house; and he had barely spoken these words
when Peter said: Here! throwing open the
door for him. A miracle it was, as great as
any, for at the imposition of his hands and the
words he uttered, Peter's wife rose from her
bed as she was bidden to do, and coming over
to Peter she asked: How shall we reward him?
and he answered her: So torn is his garment
that it trails about his feet as he walks, tripping
him; if I be fortunate with the fish to-night
I will buy him a new garment. She said:
Meanwhile I will mend his cloak for him; and
she sat down to stitch the torn parts together.
Afterwards he abode with them. For the truth
of the story I tell, Peter said to me, my good
friend

friend Barnabas will avouch, and shouldst thou wish to have further testimony, come with me to Galilee and I'll show thee the bed on which he lay, the table at which he sat, and the plate from which he ate his meat.   In my boat I will take thee over the sea of Galilee and show thee the spot where he quieted the waves that were threatening to drown us, and where we took the biggest draught of fishes ever known in those parts.   Come, stranger, I trust thee. But I said: Peter, why should I go up to Galilee?   At this question he stood abashed, saying: I thought that thou wouldst hear all I could tell thee of the Master.   All thou canst tell me of his resurrection from the dead I will hear willingly, I answered him, and from thee sooner than from another, for thou wert in Jerusalem at the time.   My reply troubled him, and wondering at his trouble, which seemed to me to be without cause, I waited till he was out of hearing to ask Barnabas to explain it to me; and his answer was that Peter was a timid man and shy, always infirm in his faith, as the Master himself knew well, for on the night before the crucifixion Jesus said to Peter: Before the cock crows thou shalt deny me thrice.   And it was so; Peter denied, and then rued his denial.   The same Peter to-day, Barnabas said, that the Master judged rightly;

he

he hath changed in nothing.   And this judgment of Peter that I received from Barnabas
was confirmed afterwards when on our return
from Cyprus, whither we had gone to preach,
we went up to Antioch, a city dear to me, for
it was there that the word Christian was spoken
for the first time.   My return was fortunate,
for there I met Barnabas, whom I rejoiced
to meet again after these many years.   All
memory of our dissensions was forgotten; we
had much to tell each other of our travels and
the conversions we had made, and our joy was
increased by Peter, who appeared amongst us,
bringing a brother with him, Silas, who must
have been grieved, though he said nothing to
me of it.   He must have seen that the law to
which he was attached was forgotten at Antioch, not by us only, but by his new leader,
Peter, who mixed like ourselves with the Gentiles and did not refuse to eat with them.   One
day we came out of a house heated with argument, and as we loitered by the pavement's edge
we came upon Peter in a public inn eating and
drinking with the uncircumcised; whereupon
the men of Jerusalem said: We see now what
thou art, Peter, a Jew that eats with Gentiles
and of unclean meats.   Peter did not withstand
them and say, as he should have done: How
is it that you call them that God hath made

unclean

unclean? but excused himself and withdrew, and was followed by Barnabas and Silas.

An angry soul I have been since God first separated me from my mother's womb, gaining something on one side and losing on another. But we make not ourselves; God makes us; and there is a jealousy still within me. I know it, and have suffered from it, and never did it cause me greater suffering than in those days in Antioch. My jealousy was like a hungry animal, gnawing at my ribs, till unable to bear it any longer, and seeing in visions all that I had raised pulled down, I started with Titus and travelled all over Galatia and Phrygia to Bithynia, founding churches everywhere I went, and everywhere persecuted by the Jews. But my life hath never been my concern but God's, a thing upheld by God for so many years that I shun danger no longer, and now it hath even come to me that I am lonely in security, withdrawn from God in houses, and safe in his arms when clinging to a spar in the dark sea. God and our Lord Jesus Christ, his beloved son, have walked on either side of me in mountain passes where robbers lie in wait. We are nearer to God in hunger and thirst than when the mouth is full, in fatigue rather than in rest, and to know oneself to be God's servant is good cheer for the traveller, better than the lights of an

inn

inn, for false brethren may await him in the inn, some that will hale him before rulers; but if he know he is God's servant he will be secure in his own heart, where alone security abides. Shipwrecked I was many times, stoned at Lystra, escaping death by feigning it, followed wherever I went by persecution from the Jews, determined to undo my work; but undeterred by stones and threats and stripes—forty save one—I returned to Lystra and preached there again, and in Perga and Attalia. From thence we returned to Antioch, and there was great rejoicing in Saigon Street when we told of the churches we had founded in Galatia, how we flung open the door of truth to the Pagans and many passed through. But what is my life to you? As I have said, it hath never been my concern, wherefore it can be no concern of yours, noble Essenes. Time never lags; I see the sand running through the glass as I speak. Not much more is left, only enough for me to tell that I would have ye meet my friends and disciples and learn from them that the revelation of the Lord Jesus of himself on the road to Damascus was not the only one. He hath appeared to his disciples many times. Witnesses abound. . . . [*He staggers into* MANAHEM'S *arms.*] Only a faintness . . . it will pass.

MANAHEM

Manahem

A cup of water!

[*One of the* Essenes *goes out and returns with a cup of water.* Manahem *holds it to* Paul's *lips.*]

Paul

Many are the revelations, but Jesus of Nazareth is the greatest and the last.

Mathias (*looking round*)

So ye would exchange the study of the Scriptures for a gospel that a misadventure on the hills hath cast among you!

Paul

My sickness is not that which overthrew me on the road to Damascus, but a faintness . . . air . . . lead me to the balcony.

[*The* Essenes *crowd round* Paul *and move towards the balcony, leaving* Mathias *and* Saddoc *in the middle of the stage.*]

Mathias

I will set a noose for him, and thou shalt see him run into it.

Saddoc

Like a foolish rabbit. And though he never comes to kick in it, I shall abide in Kerith till God calls me unto himself, the same in the end as in the beginning.

Bartholomew (*coming from the balcony*)

The schism widens every minute, and I would

would ask if Hazael should not be warned that his authority is needed here.

MATHIAS

He should indeed! [BARTHOLOMEW *makes a movement towards the inner cavern.*] Stay, Bartholomew. Art thou with us, Saddoc and I, or with Paul?

BARTHOLOMEW

I fear to break my vows, Mathias, but still greater is my fear to abide in Kerith.

[*Exit* BARTHOLOMEW.]

MATHIAS

I offer thee friendship, Saddoc, and shall not desert Kerith though the brethren leave us.

SADDOC

Thou'lt weary in Kerith without brethren to instruct in the Scriptures, and in the end wilt return to thine own Egypt. But the Lord and the Scriptures are on our side, and in the debate thy wit, Mathias—— [MATHIAS *is about to call to the* ESSENES, *but* SADDOC *stops him.*] Bartholomew hath gone to warn Hazael, and I would hear Paul confuted and overthrown in his presence.

MATHIAS

His defeat would be greater truly, but at any moment Jesus may return from the hills to guide him to Cæsarea. We may not delay. And there are other excuses for our haste.

Hazael

Hazael may be too feeble this morning to give his mind to the arguments that will be settled, for Paul is a keen debater.

MANAHEM (*from the balcony*)

And this wonderful passing of the old world was wrought by the coming of the Messiah promised beforetime, a child born of a virgin's womb!

MATHIAS (*raising his voice*)

I know of no such prediction, Manahem. The word in Isaiah is not virgin but girl, who shall conceive and bear a son and shall call his name Immanuel. In thine eagerness to accept Paul's gospel thou hast forgotten the Scriptures.

SHALLUM (*from the balcony*)

The prophecy in Deuteronomy is fulfilled in the Lord Jesus.

MATHIAS

I would answer thee, Shallum, out of Deuteronomy: The prophet that shall presume to speak a word in my name which I have not commanded him to speak, or that shall speak in the name of other Gods, even that prophet shall die.

[PAUL *and the* ESSENES *come down the stage.*]

SHALLUM (*to* ELIAKIM)

It was an act of God that separated Paul from his companion, Timothy.

ELIAKIM

ELIAKIM

And upheld him in the dangers of the path.

CALEB

Soon Jesus will return from the hills to lead him to Cæsarea, wherefore let the stranger give us instruction.

PAUL

Before I leave you I would have you learn that there is but one mediator between God and man, the Lord Jesus, and that you are free men now, the curse of the law lifted from you.

SADDOC (*aside to* MATHIAS)

The curse of the law! When he says such things it is like running a knife into me!

MATHIAS

Hush! [*To* PAUL.] The law was given to us by God.

PAUL

And hath been repealed by God, who sent his only begotten son with the joyful tidings that there is salvation for all, Jews and Gentiles alike.

MATHIAS

Thou hast fared up and down Asia for twenty years, founding churches, persecuted by the Jews and making converts among the Gentiles, which is strange—unless indeed thou wouldst maintain that the study of the Scriptures and the laws that God gave to Moses have rendered

rendered the Jews less able to receive the truth than those who worship idols.

PAUL

The conversion of the Jews was confided to Peter, that of the Gentiles to me.

MATHIAS

Already a division among you! To enlighten us thou'lt tell why the conversion of the Jews was confided to Peter?

PAUL

For that Peter and Barnabas accept circumcision. I told them at Antioch that the Gentiles would not accept circumcision, and put it to them: Can it be that God sent down his beloved son to die on the cross and be raised from the dead for no greater end than that the Jews should remain Jews and the Gentiles idolaters?

MATHIAS

Thou speakest Greek of a sort, Paul, and art specious in argument despite the rudeness of thy language.

PAUL

My language serves me well enough. My mission is among the poor and ignorant rather than among the rich.

MATHIAS

So the Christians began among the poor and uninstructed?

PAUL

PAUL

Thou wouldst not have had them begin among the wise and learned, among the Jews of Alexandria?

MATHIAS

Truly not. But a Jew of Alexandria would put to thee some simple questions which thou wouldst be troubled to answer plainly.

PAUL

Put them.

MATHIAS

A dangerous doctrine is implicit in thy gospel, Paul—that whosoever hath faith may sin and sin again, and come into salvation despite his sins. [PAUL *begins to interrupt.*] Bear with me a little while. The promise made to Moses counts for nothing?

PAUL

It counted for a great deal when we were as children lost in a desert and the law was our guide. We are no longer children, but heirs to the kingdom of heaven, Jews and Gentiles alike.

MATHIAS

The promise made to Moses was then a duplicity? [*Again* PAUL *tries to interrupt.*] Trouble not to explain, for I will pass over this matter and will ask thee instead how we may come into the faith.

PAUL

PAUL

Through grace.

MATHIAS

But how comes grace?   Whence comes it?

PAUL

Grace is a gift from God, which he gives or withholds.

MATHIAS

At his pleasure?

PAUL

Doth the vase ask the potter: Why hast thou made me thus?   Hath not the potter power over the clay to make from the same lump two vases for noble and ignoble use?

[*A murmur of approval is heard among the* ESSENES.]

MATHIAS

Hath it then come to pass that I discern a heed in the countenances around me for a potter God, a maker of things according to pattern?   [*To* PAUL.]   The Christ that possesses thee, Paul, is but the Logos, the principle that mediates between the supreme God and the world formed out of matter, which hath no being of its own, for being is not in that mere potency of all things alike, which thou callest power, but in divine reason.

PAUL

PAUL

Thou'rt nearer to Christ than thou knowest,
nearer than any of the Greeks I heard in
Athens.

MATHIAS

I gather from thy Greek that thy stay in
Athens was not long, and from thence I would
have had thee go to Alexandria, my city, to
learn philosophy from the masters. Philo
would have persuaded thee into a purer concep-
tion of God than a mere potter.

PAUL

Neither life nor death nor angels can separate me from the love of our Lord Jesus Christ.

[*Rising from his seat* MATHIAS *passes on to
the balcony and leans on the rail. The
babble of voices ceases when he holds up
his hand.*]

MATHIAS

Jesus's feet are already on the last terraces,
and in a moment he'll be knocking at our
door.

[*The door is opened by an* ESSENE.]

PAUL

He brings news of Timothy! [JESUS
*enters with a wallet over his shoulders,
carrying another in his hand. PAUL
rushes towards him.*] Before all else, thy
news of Timothy!

JESUS

JESUS

Soon after he missed thee a shepherd put him on the way to Cæsarea.

PAUL (*aside*)

For the safety of Timothy, my beloved son in the faith, I give thanks to thee, O Lord.

JESUS

Thou'lt have three days in which to thank God for the safety of Timothy. [*He hangs the wallet over* PAUL'S *shoulder.*] Cæsarea is a three-days' journey and thou'rt a tired man.

PAUL

Tired in mind rather than in body.

JESUS

I had looked forward to rousing thee myself when I returned from the hills, but I find thee disputing with the Essenes. [*To the* ESSENES.] An evil trick ye have played upon me, brethren, making it doubtful if I shall get our guest to Cæsarea in three days.

PAUL

Blame not the brethren. For remembering that I was leaving Asia for ever I could not keep back the story of him crucified——

SADDOC

Begin it not again for the sake of Jesus, lest in the telling of it the hour of departure slips by unperceived by him.

JESUS

JESUS

So the Lord Jesus was on the cross?

SADDOC (*to* PAUL)

A story hath often been told in the hills
—sometimes it is forgotten, sometimes it is
in everybody's mouth—that Jesus, the great
shepherd, was put on the cross by some Roman
Governor in Jerusalem. He will tell it to thee
on the way to Cæsarea.

PAUL (*struggling against the sickness that
is rising in him*)

So thou wert crucified, shepherd of the
Judean hills? And how didst thou escape from
the cross?

JESUS

I was raised from the tomb.

SADDOC

The hour of thy departure is nigh, Paul, but
we will send Jacob to Cæsarea——

PAUL

With news that I have worn out my strength
in argument with the Essenes?

SADDOC (*laying his hand on* PAUL's *arm*)

If I read thy face aright, the sickness is rising in thee.

PAUL

A sickness of the flesh, no more. A man is
as strong as the soul within him. Loose me,
Saddoc

Saddoc, loose me!   [*To* Jesus.]   Didst say thou wert raised from the dead by the power of the Father?

JESUS

I said I was raised from the tomb.

PAUL

He is possessed of an evil spirit!   A madman!   A madman!

[PAUL *breaks away from* SADDOC *and rushes out of the cavern.* SHALLUM, CALEB, ELEAZOR, ELIAKIM, *go on to the balcony to watch him descend the terraces.* JESUS *and* MANAHEM *remain with* SADDOC *and* MATHIAS.]

JESUS

He said: Possessed of an evil spirit.   But I am a shepherd of the hills, no more, without knowledge of him or of the dissensions he hath brought into our company.

MANAHEM

Thy words may have frightened him.

JESUS

My words were simple.   As I remember them they were: I was on the cross and was raised from the tomb.   And at these words his face changed as I have seen men's faces change at the approach of the sickness.

MANAHEM

The sickness rises in a man like a wind in

the

the air. But why did he cry: A madman! A madman! Was he possessed of a bodily or a spiritual terror?

JESUS

I must warn Hazael that our guest hath left us.

[JESUS *goes into the inner cavern and* MANA-
HEM *joins the* ESSENES *on the balcony.*]

MATHIAS (*to* SADDOC)

Hast a reason in mind for his flight?

SADDOC

His anxiety to arrive in Cæsarea according to his bond.

MATHIAS

On hearing Jesus say he was raised from the tomb Paul's disturbed brain might have begun to doubt the death and resurrection that he hath preached for the last twenty years, and in his desperation at seeing his whole life crushed like an empty eggshell underfoot strange words would come to him, and why not the words he spoke?

SADDOC

A subtle divination, Mathias—true or false, I know not which, but one that we shall be able to turn to our advantage if . . .

MATHIAS

Explain thy hesitation, Saddoc.

SADDOC

SADDOC

My thoughts were that if Paul should return to us after the seizure——

MATHIAS

Why should he return?   He will continue his journey to Cæsarea.   We are rid of him for ever.

SADDOC

Wherefore thy heart is moved with pity for a man that can no longer injure us.

MATHIAS

I am moved with pity at the thought of a man who sees his whole life crushed, as I have said, like an empty eggshell.   Many men have suffered this crucifixion, and I pity them all for reasons well known to myself.

[*Enter* HAZAEL, *leaning on* JESUS'S *arm, followed by* BARTHOLOMEW.]

HAZAEL

I have come to hear of the flight of our guest, dissensions having arisen among you. It is unfortunate——

MANAHEM (*from the balcony*)

He hath fallen on the pathway beyond the bridge, stricken!

SHALLUM (*from the balcony*)

Close by the brink, and should he stir he will fall into the brook!

HAZAEL

HAZAEL

Four of our company must go to his help with a litter.

MANAHEM

A change of bearers will be needed, for the ascent is steep, and no four men will endure it for more than two or three terraces.

HAZAEL

Thou, Manahem, and Shallum, Eleazor, Eliakim, will bear him easily across the bridge, and Bartholomew and Caleb will lend their shoulders when needed.

JESUS

I opened the door to him last night and would go to his help.

HAZAEL

I cannot spare thee, Jesus.

MANAHEM

Jacob, our shepherd, is by Paul at this moment. He leans over him, lifts him—dead man or living man I cannot say.

HAZAEL

Jacob will give his help, too, and if further help be needed he'll know where to look for it. [*The* ESSENES *come from the balcony and* HAZAEL *addresses them.*] Put all your thoughts into the saving of this man. Forget your differences, remembering that our first duty as Essenes is to succour the sick and
wounded

wounded.   I pray you to be Essenes and nothing else.   Whatever may happen afterwards is
in the mind of God.

> [*The* ESSENES *go out.*   HAZAEL *and* JESUS
> *enter the inner cavern.*   MATHIAS *and*
> SADDOC *remain.*]

CURTAIN

ACT III

A C T   I I I

SCENE: *The same. Later. When the curtain rises* MATHIAS *and* SADDOC *are dis-
covered sitting at a table talking.*

MATHIAS

THINKEST, Saddoc, that by now they
have reached the bridge-head?

SADDOC
Not yet. Methinks they should now be
about half-way down the terraces.

MATHIAS
Thy guesses are not enough, Saddoc. I need
thine eyes. Tell me, is Jacob still striving to
get Paul to his feet?
[SADDOC *rises from the table, and going to
the balcony looks over the rail.*]

SADDOC
Paul wrestles with Jacob on the path. One
or the other will fall over the brink, mayhap
both, and our trouble will be over.

MATHIAS

MATHIAS

None of our brotherhood may hope for any man's death.

SADDOC (*coming from the balcony*)

Nay, I entertained no hope of his death, but at thy request went to the balcony to report what mine eyes should see. I was of the brotherhood before thou wert, Mathias, and know the rules of our Order. [*He sits at the table.*]

MATHIAS

Saddoc, put off thy despondency. Thy wishes may be gratified yet. They are, if I read thee correctly, that Paul may be able to continue his journey and perchance find shepherds to guide him to Cæsarea, where he'll take ship. [*Pause.*] Forgive me, Saddoc, if I seemed to instruct thee. 'Twas a chance word, no more. Forget it, and return to the balcony and tell me if the litter-bearers are at the bridge-head.

SADDOC

I can tell thee without going to the balcony that they are still among the terraces. But to please thee I will report what I see. [*He goes to the balcony.*] I see Paul lying on the path by the cliff's edge quite still, and Jacob standing by. . . . Now the litter emerges from the pepper-trees. . . . Soon he'll be laid out on this very balcony, his new followers in attendance on him, listening with exalted eyes and suspended

suspended breath. His sickness will serve his heresy well!

MATHIAS

The time hath come for us to lay our heads together and discover how we may save the brethren from this interloper, this false Jew, this heretic. Were Jesus of Nazareth not amongst us we should be without the proof that cannot be denied. His hands and feet are tokens that Paul preaches a dream. [*Pause.*]

SADDOC

The plan is well laid, but . . .

MATHIAS

But what, Saddoc?

SADDOC

A man's faith is subject to his desires, and should thy plan fail and the brethren depart, there will be none left of the ancient Order of the Essenes but Hazael, Jesus, thyself and I.

MATHIAS

There'll be always broken bones among the shepherds for thee to join together, but for me there will be naught in Kerith.

SADDOC

Thou'lt return to Alexandria, whence thou camest.

MATHIAS

There is no return for me to Alexandria.

SADDOC

SADDOC

Why not, Mathias? [*A gesture from*
MATHIAS *makes plain to him that he must put
no further questions.*] Whilst I cure the sick
among the hills thou'lt sit by the brook interpreting the Scriptures to Brother Jedaiah. In
his cleft up yonder he must regret sometimes
the noise that seemed too much for him when
he was with us here.

MATHIAS

I have heard naught of him for long.

SADDOC

For three days he did not let down his basket
for food, and we thought him dead or dying,
and I went up to succour him and found him
weak but still living. He had fallen and lamed
himself, and when I had mended his leg, and
he could get about, he was again happy in his
solitude and willing to continue in it.

MATHIAS

And this is the man whom thou proposest to
me as a listener! His thoughts are in himself,
never outside of himself, just as this Paul hath
no thought for himself but for mankind,
hurrying from city to city and preaching his
doctrine of the resurrection. [*Pause.*]

SADDOC

Of what art thou thinking, Mathias? Of a
new plan to defeat Paul and to save Kerith?

MATHIAS

MATHIAS

No.   I was thinking of what my life will
be in Kerith if the brethren leave us to follow
Paul.

SADDOC

There is another future for thee, Mathias—
to write a book, for there is much wisdom in
thee.

MATHIAS

It may be that wisdom still lingers in me,
but the power to write a book is no longer
mine.

SADDOC

Often we have wondered at the fortune that
brought thee hither.

MATHIAS

And still greater would be your wonder were
I to tell how it came to pass that I left Alexandria at the height of my fame, when the city
was babbling of me and of my book, portions
of which I had begun to read at my lectures.
At first it pleased me to think modestly and to
speak modestly of myself, but as time went on
and the throng of them that came to hear
me was so great that many were turned away, it
seemed to me that all that men wished to know
unfolded itself as I wrote, and I thought of myself as one born to write this book.   I knew not
whether it would bring joy and encouragement
to

to all men; I write not as Paul speaks. The
book had life within itself, and every night
when I laid down the pen I believed that all I
had written had existed in the mind of God
from all eternity. I looked upon myself as an
instrument in the hands of God as much as Paul
doth himself. But much remained to be set
down in writing; what is not written perishes,
and death watches for every man. In the dead
of night my pen would pause, stayed by the
fear lest I might not wake up in the morning
to continue my book—men die often in their
sleep. And there was another fear; I bethought
myself how even the wise have been beguiled
by the pleasures of this world, the pleasures of
women, and I became watchful over myself,
frightened lest I might fall into the pit that
other men had fallen into. Soberly as I live,
I said to myself, I may fall from this life of
moderation and chastity; philosophy may no
longer be enough. The flesh may overpower
the mind in me as it hath in other men. For
the sake of my book I must make myself safe
against danger. This thought became fixed;
I could not escape from it; and there were
wandering spirits, all determined on my over-
throw. A voice spake within me: There is
but one way; sacrifice thy manhood. I had
seen youths in the temple of Ashtoreth sacrifice

fice their manhood with sharp shells. I did likewise. . . .

SADDOC

And having rid thyself of these beguilements, did thy book prosper?

MATHIAS (*starting to his feet*)

Why torment me with questions?

SADDOC

Thy choice, Mathias, was to open thy heart to me, and being a physician, a healer——

MATHIAS

We cannot separate the body from the soul without loss to one or the other. As I lay rejoicing in the thought that I could now write what would outlast time itself, I felt suddenly —a spasm of thought it was—that my book no longer lived from itself, and when I went to it words failed me, or was there no thought to sustain the words? My thought dissolved in images and I wrote on, believing I had accomplished something, but when I returned to what I had written there were on the page only words, nothing of what I would have written. And after vain efforts of many months I said: The spirit will never again awaken in me; I am dead; and going to a friend I told him my story. He reminded me how I had spoken the day before in the school, how all had listened entranced to my eloquence, and I answered:

Only

Only eloquence remains, mists of words seemingly beautiful in themselves but which have no substance. Here is my manuscript, I continued; do with it what thou wilt, but let no man know that I have given it. Next day I departed for Lower Egypt, where as thou knowest there are Essenes; but the heat of their rocky solitudes was too great for my health, and looking northward I came to Kerith. Such is my story, Saddoc, and I would ask what conclusion thou drawest from it.

SADDOC

Thou shalt die here in Kerith, and be buried under the rocks within hearing of the brook's threnody. Hearken to it, Mathias! It goes by whispering some great secret plainly enough.

MATHIAS

But if we ask ourselves what the brook is saying we get no answer. We hear only water going by. . . . There comes a trampling of feet!

SADDOC

The litter-bearers are coming up the last terrace.

[*They listen for a moment. Enter the litter-bearers with* PAUL.]

DIFFERENT ESSENES

Not here. . . . No, not there. . . . On the balcony, where the air is fresher.

[*The* ESSENES *carry* PAUL *to the balcony and*
lay

lay him on a bench amid a murmur of voices.]

SADDOC (*to* BARTHOLOMEW)

Hath he spoken?

BARTHOLOMEW

He murmured and raved incontinently as we came up the terraces.

SADDOC

Do thou go and fetch a basin of water and some cloths.

[*Exit* BARTHOLOMEW. *A pause.* PAUL *rouses a little.*]

CALEB (*to* PAUL)

On seeing thee fall we ran without stopping till we came to the bridge.

MANAHEM (*mopping his brow*)

As nimbly as we might with the litter. The descent is only a thought easier than the ascent.

ELIAKIM

'Twas a stiff climb truly.

CALEB (*to* PAUL)

To ensure thine ease we changed bearers at every terrace.

MANAHEM

My shoulder saith not so, Caleb. I bore him for three without a change.

SHALLUM

And I still feel his weight after one!

MANAHEM

MANAHEM

And my shoulder was again under the litter when we set him down here.

[SADDOC *goes to* PAUL *and feels his pulse.* BARTHOLOMEW *enters with a basin of water and a cloth, which he hands to* SADDOC.]

SADDOC

In a few minutes he'll be himself again. [*He bathes* PAUL's *temples.*]

MATHIAS

Ready to begin the journey to Cæsarea?

SADDOC

Hush!   Speak not of Cæsarea.   He may awaken at the word, and I would have him sleep a while longer.   [*Enter* HAZAEL, *supported by* JESUS. SADDOC *goes forward to meet them.*] A man may rise from these fits and continue his work without knowledge of what hath befallen him, or he may lie helpless for a day, or even two.

HAZAEL (*looking towards the balcony*)

If he awaken now, will he be able for the journey?

MATHIAS

In case of a lesser seizure, his guide will know where to find him shelter.

HAZAEL

Go, Eleazor, and bid Jacob hold himself in readiness.

[*Exit* ELEAZOR.]

SADDOC

Saddoc

Thou dost well to choose Jacob, Hazael.
'Twere hard for thee that Jesus should leave
thee on the day after his return.

Hazael

Speak not of myself. It is our brotherhood
that is divided between me and yon man who
lieth stricken in sickness.

Mathias

If we would save Kerith we must cast out
Paul.

Saddoc

Let me speak now, Hazael, no longer as a
physician. It is not meet that Paul should
leave us until he and all the brethren have
heard from Jesus the story of his crucifixion.

Hazael

Our rule disfavours any inquisition into the
past life of one of our brethren, but be it
now as ye will. Speak truly, Jesus, if thou
wouldst help us in our strait.

Mathias, Saddoc and the Others

Speak, Jesus!

Jesus

I had a purpose to speak when I returned
hither yesterevening, and I sought counsel con-
cerning it with Hazael. I could not remain,
I told him, without revealing how I came to
break my vows. He urged that there is much
disquiet

disquiet in Kerith, that old stories would only add to the confusion, and begged that I should be silent. And unable to withstand his pleading, I said: Be it so. But since these words were spoken a man hath come amongst us with a story that Jesus of Nazareth was raised from the dead by the power of the Father and spoke to him out of the clouds, and if it may allay the perplexities that have arisen thereby in our community I will now declare that I myself was born in Nazareth and followed Hazael to Kerith. How it came that I left him I need not delay to tell, save only this, that I received baptism from John, and like him preached the gospel of repentance. My preaching was received with joy and acclaim along the shores of the lake by the fishermen and by many from Tiberias, and miracles were performed by me, for at that time the power of God wrought in me—there is no power in the world but God's. I speak not now vaingloriously, but confess to you that at that time I was puffed up with pride and arrogance. I forgot God and went down to Jerusalem expecting a great welcome. On an ass richly caparisoned I rode into the city, the people strewing palms before me and crying Hosannas, and when some reproved them for so doing, I said: If they did not proclaim me the stones themselves would

would do so. [*The* ESSENES *murmur amongst themselves.*] Unwilling that your eyes should look upon a blasphemer you cover your faces with your hands, and you would seal your ears if you could against the story I am telling. . . . In Jerusalem I said I could destroy the temple and build it up again in three days, and my words coming to the ears of the High Priest, Caiaphas, he sent his servants in search of me. I was taken in a garden whither I had gone to pray and was brought before the High Priest, who questioned me and tore his hair and cried: A blasphemer! Pilate was my judge, and the punishment he meted out to me was a scourging and the carrying of my cross to Golgotha. Qn it I hung till I passed into a swoon, and being deemed dead at the end of the third hour, my body was given to Joseph of Arimathea for burial. [PAUL, *rousing, listens intently.*] He laid me in the tomb that he had had carved for himself, and as he was about to close it I stirred in my grave-clothes, and seeing I was not dead he carried me to his house, where I remained till my wounds were cured. When I was able to move about I worked in the olive garden, carrying faggots and pruning the trees, my wits happily away, till the smell of a camel-driver recalled the hills, and henceforth I could wonder only if my my flock was thriving or wasting under Brother Amos's care. [*At this moment his eyes fall on* PAUL.] See, Paul listens. His wits are returning to him.

MATHIAS

He hath missed nothing.

PAUL

A strange story indeed, and well worth the hearing, so truthfully is it told.

MATHIAS

As well worth the hearing as the voice that spoke to thee out of the clouds, Paul, and should a memory of that voice still haunt in thee, we shall be glad to hear if thou canst distinguish a sameness in the two voices.

PAUL

Thy words enter my ears, Mathias, but for what thou intendest——

SADDOC

Brethren, crowd not about him. Let him enjoy the air of the balcony till he is rested and his mind composed.

MANAHEM

We would hear what he hath to say ere he leaves us at midday.

SADDOC

He dozes, and must not be awakened. Mayhap sleep will bring him into his full mind, and then you can put questions to him.

MANAHEM

MANAHEM

Thou shouldst have been with us, Mathias, when he spake to us on the balcony. His words fixed themselves in the memory of his hearers for ever.

MATHIAS

I would hear the words that are fixed in thy memory for ever, Manahem.

MANAHEM

Not in my memory alone, but perchance in the memory of all men. Even thou wouldst have been exalted hadst thou heard him speak. [*Murmuring to himself*.] When I was a child I spoke as a child, I understood as a child, I thought as a child; but when I became a man I put away childish things.

PAUL (*rousing*)

Brethren, I hear your voices. . . . Saddoc and Manahem were in dispute, and then my wit slumbered. But now it wakes, and I remember that my day among you is shortening. Question me.

MATHIAS

We disputed which was the true Jesus, he whom thou teachest or the Jesus that heretofore hath led our flocks home. So alike are their stories that we are perplexed. Our brother Jesus preached in Galilee and was crucified in Jerusalem twenty years agone, and it was at that

that time that thy Jesus of Nazareth spoke to
thee out of the clouds. Wherefore either a
great miracle or a great deception is wrapped
up in thy teaching, and we would hear from
thee, who hast seen and heard both the dead
and the quick, which we should follow.

PAUL

Thou wast a listener when I told my story,
how after three years spent in Arabia I went up
to Jerusalem and spoke with Peter, the Lord's
Apostle, and with James, the brother of the
Lord. Wherefore I guess thee to be a caviller,
one who would take advantage of my plight.
But I would not have thy questions refused an
answer. A long journey awaits me——

MATHIAS

A single question and its answer will free
us from doubt. Which Jesus is the Messiah
promised to the Jews?

PAUL

The Lord Jesus Christ, who sits in heaven by
the side of the Father. Jesus, thy shepherd,
liveth before me in the flesh.

MATHIAS

Before thy seizure he was declared to be
possessed of an evil spirit. A madman! was thy
cry. We would hear if thou holdest by these
words. [*Turning to the* ESSENES.] When the
mind darkens in sickness the truth slips out.

PAUL

PAUL

To hide my sickness from you I ran away. All else is forgotten.

MATHIAS

We have the witness of our brother's hands and feet.

PAUL (*rising with an effort*)

I have no need to look into his hands and feet for the scars of his crucifixion. He was on the cross, I deny it not, like many another, and escaped death as some have done. The man liveth for examination. Look into his eyes; touch his hands and face. [*Suddenly becoming calm.*] Thou art a philosopher from Alexandria, Mathias, and judgest all things by the light of reason; wherefore examine the story with which thou wouldst confute me, and tell me if it be within the purposes and devices of the Father that his son should be crucified and raised from the dead for no further end than to lead flocks from pasture to pasture, keeping the great truth buried in his breast that there is salvation for all. Thou wouldst have done well to have put these questions to thyself before coming to me for answers.

MATHIAS

Nay, look thou into the shepherd's hands and feet and thou'lt read testimony that he was on the cross.

PAUL

PAUL

As to that, have not my words been clear?

HAZAEL

Jesus, I would hear thee speak.   Hast thou naught to say in this dispute?

JESUS

Perchance Paul knoweth of another Jesus, the Christ———

PAUL

Yea, him that was raised from the dead and will remain till the last man perishes, to be united then to the Father which is in heaven, and henceforth there will be but one God.

JESUS

It may be that my name hath been mingled with these happenings, whatsoever they were. I know not.   Nor do I doubt that a voice spoke to Paul out of the skies.   He that walks with God will hear his voice.   To some it is a thunderbolt from the heavens, to some it is a voice that speaks from within, but every man that prayeth well may hear the voice of the Father. He that hath ears to hear will hear.   It may be, as I have said, that my name hath crept into these reports, and that my sufferings, which were great, have been used by God for his own glory.   [*He smiles.*]   Paul, I would not rob thee of my namesake!

MATHIAS

MATHIAS

That is well spoken, Jesus! Wisdom hath uttered a voice even among the Gentiles, to Socrates, to Pythagoras. Nay, I myself, did I not once hear a voice?

PAUL

Thou speakest, Mathias, after the wisdom of Egypt, in empty phrases, to withdraw the thoughts of the brethren from the miracle of the resurrection. The Greeks seek after wisdom, but the need of all peoples is a miracle. They hearkened unto me in Athens till I began to speak of the resurrection, whereupon they jeered, crying out that no man was ever raised from the dead. And I returned to Asia cast down by the thought of the great numbers that would die without knowledge of the Lord Jesus, however long I might live, however far I might travel. O, my Lord Jesus, I cried, I would hold myself accursed for the sake of my brethren, my kinsmen according to the flesh; and remembering that I was within twenty leagues of Jericho, I went to the noble Festus to ask for six days' absence from Cæsarea to preach in Jericho. The journey to Jericho is now over, and my feet are already on the way to Rome. Three days hence I shall be in Cæsarea, in a month in Rome, preaching my gospel without fear of persecution by the Jews.

SHALLUM

SHALLUM

And after Rome?

PAUL

Spain.

MANAHEM

And after Spain thou'lt return to Asia to take account of our stewardship.

ELIAKIM

Whilst thou art absent in Rome and in Spain we shall found many churches, and a great welcome will be given to thee on thy return. In my thoughts I can see the converts crowding round, welcoming the Apostle of the Gentiles.

MANAHEM

The seed hath been sown.

PAUL

But he who hath sown will not garner.

MANAHEM

Thou wilt not die in Spain.

PAUL

How knowest thou? My sleep is often broken by a dream in which I behold myself striking in haste across a rocky plain towards mountains which lie afar off. As my strength departs the Lord Jesus comes to my help, and I cry: Give me strength to reach the village beyond the mountains and to preach thy

resurrection

resurrection, and salvation through thee, for, my Lord Jesus, they are guiltless—thy name hath never reached their ears; it is but just that they should hear it. The world perishes year by year; in a few it will be gone. My dear Lord Jesus, thy servant comes to thee at the end of a long day, weary of the world but refreshed by sight of thee, and still ardent to bring the innocent of law and sin to salvation. Bend down, Lord Jesus, till I see thee, whom I have seen so often in sleeping, in waking, in perils in the sea, in deserts——

MATHIAS

Belike it will be another shepherd lad, Paul, bending over thee, to give thee to drink from his gourd——

[*Enter* ELEAZOR, *followed by* JACOB *carrying two wallets.* HAZAEL *and* JESUS *retire into the inner cavern.*]

JACOB (*to* PAUL)

Master, art thou ready? When Eleazor brought me now Hazael's message, bidding me guide thee to Cæsarea: It cannot be, I said, that he can start without another night's rest!

PAUL

Do always as thou art bidden to do, Jacob.

JACOB

Here then is thy wallet, with food for three days

days. [*To* SADDOC.] Hath he strength for so long a journey?

SADDOC

No other ill but weariness can I find in him, a profound weariness.

JACOB

We shall sleep in caves on soft sand. If go he must we should go now.

PAUL

My promise is given, or I would remain with you a little longer, for much hath been left unsaid that should have been said. I would speak to you of good will to one's neighbour, of affection one to another, and of many other things. But Jacob's eyes are upon me. [*He turns to go.*] Farewell, brethren. Stop on the roads now and then to speak of me. Think of me in Italy, and afterwards in Spain by the great sea that no man knows the end of. Each man here hath a trade and he will live by it, accepting bread from no man but living by the work of his hands, as I have lived. Think of all that is lovely, of all that is pure, of things that are kind, of things that are good. Avoid the blasphemous and the evil-living——

JACOB

Paul——

PAUL

Good-bye, brethren, whom I shall never see again

again in the flesh, mayhap, but whom I shall always see with the eyes of the spirit. I salute you all, even Saddoc and Mathias, who would have caused division between us. I bear no grudge to them. The truth will be revealed to them by the Lord Jesus himself in good time. I thank you for the food I have had and the bed I have slept in. . . . My spirit is bowed down, but go I must. Even Timothy I cannot bring with me. He returns to Derbe, to his mother, to preach the gospel to the idolaters of that city, and you, Manahem, Bartholomew, Shallum, Eliakim, Eleazor, Caleb, will preach in Macedonia, Thessalonica, Galatia. In Corinth you will meet Aquila and Priscilla, faithful servants whom ye will greet in friendship and with a holy kiss. There is Apollos, too, and many another. Their names crowd upon me, but of what avail were it to speak them now? They would pass out of your memory. I will write to you from Rome.

[PAUL *goes out, followed by* JACOB. SADDOC *and* MATHIAS *remain apart, and the* ESSENES, *with the exception of* MANAHEM, *crowd on to the balcony.*]

SHALLUM

He strides away like a shepherd, and last night was the first for many nights that he slept in a bed.

ELIAKIM

ELIAKIM

Already we are forgotten.

BARTHOLOMEW

Not forgotten. We shall be with him in his prayers, and he'll be with us in ours.

[*Exeunt* SADDOC *and* MATHIAS.]

ELEAZOR

Come to the balcony, Manahem, if thou wouldst see him for the last time.

MANAHEM (*crossing to the balcony and speaking with his hand on* SHALLUM'S *shoulder*)

At every stride he grows smaller in our eyes and greater in our hearts.

SHALLUM

After Rome he will take ship for Spain.

MANAHEM

But not to die. He will return to us, and a joyful day it will be when he visits the churches we have founded and sees the converts we bring to him.

SHALLUM

Thou speakest well, Manahem. Henceforth we are no longer Essenes but Christians, and the doctrine we preach shall be the doctrine we have received from Paul.

ELIAKIM

His eyes were upon me when he spoke of
Corinth

Corinth, and his voice was addressed to me when he said: Aquila and Priscilla you will meet in Corinth, and they will instruct you more fully than I can before my departure.

ELEAZOR
I heard him say none of these things to thee, Eliakim. Methought when he spoke of Corinth that his eyes were upon me.

MANAHEM
Remember his words, that there should be no envyings amongst us. [*Pause.*] He hath passed under the overhanging rock.

CALEB
Yes; but we can overtake him if we hasten.

MANAHEM
Then let us hasten, for the instructions he hath given us are not sufficient. Dissensions may arise amongst us. Let us hasten. We shall overtake him before he hath reached the level road.

[*The* ESSENES *go out hurriedly. Enter* JESUS, *leading* HAZAEL.]

JESUS
Here is thy chair.

HAZAEL
Are the brethren all gone?

JESUS
Be thou seated and I will go to the balcony
and

and make count of them as they descend the terraces. [*He goes on to the balcony and looks over the rail.*]

HAZAEL

How many of our brethren follow Paul?

JESUS

Saddoc and Mathias are not among them.

HAZAEL

Then we shall be four in Kerith.

JESUS (*crossing to the other side of the balcony*)

Saddoc and Mathias are in the path down which I came last night with Jacob. Walking studiously, they consider how the brotherhood of the Essenes may be saved.

HAZAEL

Thinkest, Jesus, that the brethren can be persuaded to return to Kerith?

JESUS

In three days Paul will be on board a Roman ship.

HAZAEL

But his Apostles will remain in Asia.

[*Footsteps are heard outside. Enter* MATHIAS *and* SADDOC.]

MATHIAS

In a few minutes the brethren will overtake the new prophet.

SADDOC

SADDOC

And before they reach Cæsarea we shall have already made a laughing-stock of Paul's doctrine in Jerusalem.

HAZAEL

And how may ye accomplish this?

MATHIAS

If Jesus will come with us it will be easy. [*Turning to* JESUS.] Have no fear, Jesus, for thyself. Thy reception will be a great one. The past will be undone, and the High Priest will send servants to Rome to confute Paul in thy name.

JESUS

I stumbled once in the belief that we who did not make the world can remake it, but I have learnt since that the world is ever in the hands of God. He is moulding it always, without our help and warily.

MATHIAS

Thou art not with us, then?

JESUS

I am neither with you nor against you. [*Exeunt* MATHIAS *and* SADDOC.] They go in such haste to confound the errors of men that Brother Jedaiah's basket of food is forgotten. I will take it to him. [*He picks up the basket.*] Mayhap they will learn in time that
it

it is better to love the good than to hate the
wicked.

> [JESUS *goes out.* . HAZAEL *falls on his knees
> and prays.*]

CURTAIN